The Empowered Teen

The ultimate resource for self-discovery,
driving you towards your dream career.

Written By

Markus De Silva

The Empowered Teen

ISBN 978-0-244-50279-9

www.markusdesilva.com

"Dreams are achievable, but you have to believe that it is possible and you must be willing to do the work!"

-

Markus De Silva

CONTENTS

INTRODUCTION

As you all know, thinking about what you want to become or do with yourself upon leaving school can sometimes be a daunting task.

Recent studies now indicate, that the majority of school leavers do not know what it is that they would like to do after finishing school and I know from personal experience that even though the options seem endless, finding a career path that suits is often quite hard to do.

It is true that we are all predestined to leave school and go into the workforce. I mean after all, we all need to survive in this ever-changing world and unfortunately most of the things that we need in order to achieve this are centered around the ability to make money.

I would hate for you to adopt an unrealistic mindset or a lifestyle based around money alone. It has been said that money can't buy happiness, however we should all be learning to use money as a tool to get the things we need in life.

Accumulating wealth can come from so many different avenue streams, but why work a mundane or boring nine to five job when whilst your young and have time on your side, you can map out your options and be happy from the get go when transitioning from school leaver and into your adult lives.

It is my goal to write this resource to share with you my own experiences, as well as to encourage you to answer a few simple questions with the hope that you will finish this book with a clear indication of what it is that you would like to pursue as you draw near the end of finishing High School.

This book will only work if you take the time to complete each of the "Chapter Challenges" that are set out before you. With these challenges I will ask that you really take the time to think about your answers as this will reveal to you what it is that you have always enjoyed doing and also will open up the doors into the areas of work/experiences that you are more than interested in.

So without wasting anymore time, let's jump right in to Chapter One.

Markus De Silva

www.markusdesilva.com

CHAPTER ONE

"Who are you in school?"

When I was younger and in school, there were certain subjects that really stood out to me. I remember loving both English and Science, and also being involved in music. Even though I enjoyed other things like sports and woodwork, it was really those three subjects that I was more interested in than the rest.

You see, English class for me was all about reading and writing. I loved putting pen to paper and as you are now reading for yourself, writing enables me to not only get creative at times but also to share my message with the world. Writing is easily one of my passions and I never really realized this for quite some time whilst going through life as a young adult.

Maybe this is the nerd in me but seriously, who doesn't love science. I really enjoyed science and mainly the study of animals. I grew up in a small coastal community, literally right on the beach and every chance I had I was running through the bush or sand dunes looking for the local wildlife. I always had pets growing up and each of my science projects were always based around animals. Clearly, this is another school subject that I enjoyed.

I also now believe that music is the universal language. Whether you love "pop" or "punk rock", music makes you feel things without you even realizing it.

You would know yourselves how music can make you feel when you begin listening to it. We each have our favorite artists or songs and these are unique to each of us and for a reason. Music is relatable, the message is easy to understand and sometimes, the artist is singing exactly what it is that you may have just needed to hear.

Music is so much a passion of mine, that through my late teenage and young adult years I played in a band and got to have some pretty amazing experiences. I have been able to record songs and release albums, feature on other musician's releases and I have made some great friendships along the way.

I hope that just by reading through my top three, you will see how much all three of these subjects have meant to me. These are the subjects that I should have followed a career path into after leaving school, because if I had done that I wouldn't have wasted some much time floundering through my younger adult years of life, working in jobs that really didn't mean all that much to me.

It is important for you to have a clear indication as to what it is that you are interested in whilst at school. Your school years should be helping you become the adult that you want to be and therefore I believe that High School is a major contributing factor to your future working career. So please don't take it lightly.

I know of countless others, who just like myself have left or continue to leave school without a clear career direction of what they would like to pursue. And I can say from personal experience and on behalf of these people, that this has resulted in a lot of wasted time and going through life feeling unfulfilled.

I believe that there should be more resources available to you all whilst you are nearing finishing High School, and that is the main reason why I have written this book for you.

This is the resource that I wish I had back when I was younger, as I would have understood more clearly about which career choices I should have pursued.

So let's jump into the Chapter Challenge.

CHAPTER ONE

"Challenge"

I am now going to ask you to think about and write down your top three subjects whilst at school.

Please remember to give these some thought and to focus your thinking on which of those subjects you are most interested in.

Even though you may like more than three subjects, there are bound to be three of them that you really strive to excel in.

What are my top three subjects at school that I am most interested in?

(Your Answers)

1.

2.

3.

Now I would like you to take some time and write down why these top three subjects that you have chosen really interest you.

Please refer to my top three if needed and write a small paragraph for each of your own answers in the space provided below.

(Your Answers)

1. I really enjoy ………. (insert subject) at school, because ……….

2. I really enjoy ………. (insert subject) at school, because ……….

3. I really enjoy ………. (insert subject) at school, because ……….

CHAPTER TWO

"Who are you at home?"

When I wasn't at school and I didn't have any family commitments to attend to, I had hobbies that I enjoyed and lost track of time whilst doing. Everyone has these and usually we have one or two that really take the cake and stand out from the rest.

These are usually known as your passions or outside interests. They can be something that you may want to pursue or activities that you will still partake in whilst working in another area.

For me, I really love fishing. As I have mentioned previously, I grew up on the coast and fishing was an important part of that lifestyle. My Dad actually taught me how to fish and to this day, the techniques that I have learnt from him I now pass down to my own sons who seem to be showing the same interest and taking a strong liking to fishing for themselves.

Fishing is a hobby of mine that I love to do whenever I get the chance. Even though I know that I do not want to become a commercial fisherman or even that I want to do it as a full-time job, I really enjoy it as a recreational hobby. Whether the fish are biting or not, the whole point of it is to get out there and to lose track of time whilst doing something that I enjoy.

For you, your hobbies may include playing an instrument, playing a sport or even participating in a local community group. This does not mean that you have to go on to take a job in any of these areas, but understanding your hobbies will help to further define who you are and what you are interested in. And this is extremely important to figure out so that when the time comes and you do go on to working in your adult lives, you can obtain a healthy work-life balance that so many others out there are currently struggling to achieve.

You see, it is crucial that even as an adult you continue to do the things that you enjoy. Most adults go into their working lives and forget about the "fun stuff", and this should not be the case. I mean yes we all have to work or make money in order to provide but being mentality and physically happy is also just as important.

Even now, you may find that as you move towards you final years of school you can become overwhelmed. You may already have ways to deal with the stress, such as going out with friends or choosing to partake in an activity that enables you to take your mind of things for a while. If this is you, please continue to do this as you are on the right path to becoming a well-balanced adult. And if this is not you, please make an effort to start.

So again, without wasting anymore time, let's jump right in to Chapter Challenge.

CHAPTER TWO

"Challenge"

I am now going to ask you to think about and write down your top two hobbies/interests.

Please remember to give these some thought and to focus your thinking on which of these hobbies/interests you find yourself losing track of time in whilst doing.

Even though you may have more than two, there are bound to be two of them that you really enjoy and that stand out.

What are my top two hobbies/interests that I find myself losing track of time in whilst enjoying to do?

(Your Answers)

1.

2.

Now I would like you to take some time and write down why these top two that you have chosen really interest you.

(Your Answers)

1. I really enjoy ………. (insert hobby) at home, because ……….

2. I really enjoy ………. (insert hobby) at home, because ……….

CHAPTER THREE

"What is my Vision of Self?"

I love the term, "Vision of Self". If three words could wear a halo, these would be them.

These three words mean so much to me as while I was growing up, I never had a clear vision of who I was, what I wanted to be or how I was going to achieve my own goals.

It is so important and even more so that throughout your teenage years you have a clear and well-defined "Vision of Self".

Your vision should include things like your health goals, your lifestyle goals, your activity goals and your overall bigger picture.

A great and personal "Vision of Self" builds confidence and establishes direction in one's life. It will help you to understand that as human beings, we are each unique and individual.

There is nothing wrong with someone else's lifestyle choices being different to your own. And even though we may not fully understand why someone else behaves or does something that we may not always agree with, that's totally ok and we need to be cool with that.

As grounded and mature young adults, we need to practice the age-old saying of "treating people the way that we ourselves want to be treated".

Each and every one of us out there deserves respect and consideration in our day to day lives. And as you grow up and get older, you don't have to like everyone and again, that is totally ok.

You will find that you will naturally gravitate towards the people that inspire and encourage you to want to change and to achieve greater things for your own life.

As an adult, I can tell you that life can seem hard and you will most definitely encounter difficult times and situations along the way. But it is important to note that it is how you react to these situations that will define your character and this is a really valuable piece of advice that I would like you all to remember.

They say that "if you don't laugh, you cry", and this is true for most things. So don't sweat the small stuff as tomorrow will always bring forth a new day and present with it new opportunities.

Let's jump in to Chapter Challenge.

CHAPTER THREE

"Challenge"

(My Example)

My "Vision of Self" is to be confident, happy and healthy.

I understand that people are different, and that I am unique and an individual.

My goals are to be motivated and successful.

I would love to leave school and become either a writer or science teacher, or even work in the field of environmental conservation.

I have dreams of writing a best selling novel or even playing on a main stage with a band, however I am content and committed to living my life to it's fullest.

I would now really like for you to write down a clear "Vision of Self" that speaks to your heart. This may take a couple of attempts to get right, however the main point of the exercise is just to start.

Your vision may not be exactly what you want it to be to begin with and that's ok. As you work through the rest of the chapter challenges within this book, you can change your vision at any time to suit.

Please use my vision as an example and change my answers to whatever it is that you would like it to say.

I have also included the following template to assist you if required.

(Your Answers)

My "Vision of Self" is to be ……….., ……….. and ………..

I understand that people are different, and that I am unique and an individual.

My goals are to be ……….. and ………..

I would love to leave school and become either a ……….. or ……….., or even work in the field of ………………..

I have dreams of ……….. or even ……….., however I am content and committed to living my life to it's fullest.

CHAPTER FOUR

"Achieving my Vision of Self"

Now, this is where we begin mapping out how we can make our visions start working for each and every one of us. This process should be an exciting time, as in order to achieve your own vision I will show you exactly how easy it is to start and to follow on with. Let's get to it and use my own vision as the example.

My first sentence in my vision was *"to be confident, happy and healthy."*

This opening sentence for me personally, really sums up overall how I want to see myself. It is so easy to get caught up and distracted in other things or someone else's ideal vision for our lives and even though it is great to respect other people's opinions, what we now go on to do and achieve after leaving High School is totally our own responsibility.

When I left school, I remember neither feeling confident, happy or really that healthy. If anything, I was always a slim kid and that hasn't changed even in my adult years. All my friends at school were much bigger than me and because I thought that was "normal" I gave myself a really hard time about it.

I never went swimming in High School. I was always embarrassed about being smaller than everyone else and I never understood that we are each unique to our own shape at the time. This really bothered me because I wanted to be like everyone else, however now as an adult I have realized that my goal of being "fit" really does not need to be the same as anyone else's.

I was also never really happy at school because one, I never really knew what it was that I wanted to do and two, I never really grasped that school was going to prepare me in some way, shape or form for my adult working life.

Who thinks of their health when their 15. Everyone I knew in school didn't seem to care about the repercussions of anything they were partaking in, let alone what the long-term effects may be.

This is a huge problem that we have today and one that must also be addressed. As teenagers and young adults, you should be confident, happy and healthy. You shouldn't have to conform to what society or "Hollywood" may be trying to tell us is beautiful as we are each unique to our own shapes and beliefs.

Confidence must start from within. It's a mental game that you must get right in your head before allowing yourself into being fooled by the world's opinions.

Confidence starts with self-belief. If your thoughts become your actions, then your actions define your character. Your habits and personality traits that you are showing now, will carry over into your adult years of life, so getting them right now is really important as first impressions can be everything.

As an adult, it has taken me years to come to peace with my slim build. I struggled with it for so long and I was always trying to understand why I couldn't gain or put on the extra muscle like all of my other friends. As it turns out, my goals in this area of my life were completely messed up and wrong.

You see, my Father has the exact same build as me. And rather then me factor my genetics into the equation, I began training and trying to eat like all of my friends that were so much bigger than me. After years of trying and after a lot of frustration, this then resulted in a major light-bulb moment.

First off, I realized that I didn't want to live in the gym nor did I even like going there. I preferred to work out at home and I still do to this day, but the "gym" lifestyle just didn't interest me at all.

Secondly, I realized that I have no desire to eat the amount of food each day that it would take to look like that. I honestly just don't have the time or stomach for it and therefore I had initially established an unrealistic goal to begin with, which in turn enabled me to set myself up for failure without knowing it at the time.

After beating myself up about not looking a certain way for so long, I now have to wonder why I did that? My answer would be by saying that I did it to feel like I would be accepted. I did it to feel normal. However no one tells you at the time that what is normal for someone else is not necessarily normal for you.

You see, regardless of my size I am normal. And now after realizing this, my health goals have changed and I love it!

I still aim to work out at least three times a week, but I don't do it in the gym. I love the simplicity of body weight training (like pushups, pull-ups, etc) and this works for me and for my lifestyle.

My ideal body goals are now more realistic for my natural shape and rather then want to look like "The Hulk", I now want to look like Bruce Lee (you may have to google him if your not old enough to already have been a fan, lol).

I wanted to share all this with you because you can all do the same. You should all have a healthy version of yourself that you would like to achieve and it should be realistic and in line with your natural shape.

The goal in all of this is to be "fit and not fat". And everyone's version of "fit" will vary, depending on their goals.

So let's get to work and I'll show you how it easy it is to set your own goals in this area of your life.

CHAPTER FOUR

"Challenge"

I am now going to break down and drill further into my own answers to highlight how I can now goal set and achieve this in my own day to day life.

1. In order for me to be confident, I need to …

Be happy with the way I look.

Understand that everyone is different and that I may not look like what other people want me to look like.

I know that I am unique, special and that I have self-worth.

I love who I am and how I look.

The way I carry and present myself to others represents who I am as a person.

I take care of myself and keep myself clean (personal hygiene).

I may not know all the answers, however I am more than happy to ask questions when and if needed.

2. In order for me to be happy, I need to ...

Understand what makes me happy, whether that may be my family, school or my hobbies.

Make the time to do the things that I enjoy on a regular basis.

Spend more time with my family and friends.

Not let the small things blow out of proportion and get the better of me.

Realize that tomorrow is another day and will bring forth brand new opportunities for me and my future.

3. In order for me to be healthy, I need to ...

Make smarter food choices.

Understand what certain food/s does to me body.

Make sure that I get a minimum of 7 hours sleep each night.

Make sure that I don't have any screen time at least one hour before bed.

Exercise at least three times each week.

Have friends and people around me that encourage and inspire me to want more out of life.

Have genuine, supportive and loving relationships with those around me.

As you can now begin to see, in order for me to start living my life according to my vision, I need to start doing the things that I have myself highlighted in my answers.

It might seem like this is common sense, however having to think about it and write it down in a easy to follow guide not only empowers us moving forward but also enables us to go back, review and keep things on track if we ever start to feel that we are slowing drifting off our predestined paths to greatness.

It's important to note that when writing your goals, they should also be measurable. This means that each of your goals should include a completion date and any further steps that may be required to achieve them. (This will be further detailed in Chapter Nine, where I will give you a goal setting example that I actually use myself).

We are now going to work through each of the sentences of your vision over the next couple of pages and to begin, I will ask that you break down your first sentence just as I have done on the templates below.

PART A (Please fill in the blank spaces with your answers from your vision)

My "Vision of Self" is to be ………., ………., and ……….

In order for me to be ………., I need to …

1.

2.

3.

4.

5

In order for me to be ...., I need to ...

1.
2.
3.
4.
5.

In order for me to be ...., I need to ...

1.
2.
3.
4.
5.

PART B (Please fill in the blank spaces with your answers from your vision)

"I understand that people are different, and that I am unique and an individual."

Please take a moment to really think about what this sentence means to you and write down the first thing that comes to mind in the space provided below.

PART C (Please fill in the blank spaces with your answers from your vision)

My goals are to be ………. and ……….

In order to achieve my goal of ………. I need to ...

1.
2.
3.
4.
5.

In order to achieve my goal of ………. I need to …

1.
2.
3.
4.
5.

PART D (Please fill in the blank spaces with your answers from your vision)

I would love to leave school and become either a ………. or ……….., or even work in the field of ………………..

In order for me to become a ………. I need to …

1.

2.

3.

4.

5.

In order for me to become a ………. I need to …

1.

2.

3.

4.

5.

In order for me to work in the field of ……….. I need to …

1.
2.
3.
4.
5.

PART E (Please fill in the blank spaces with your answers from your vision)

I have dreams of ……….. or even ……….., however I am content and committed to living my life to it's fullest.

In order to achieve my dream of ………. I need to …

1.

2.

3.

4.

5.

In order to achieve my dream of ………. I need to …

1.

2.

3.

4.

5.

PART F (Please fill in the blank spaces with your answers from your vision)

"I am content and committed to living my life to it's fullest".

Please take a moment to really think about what this sentence means to you and write down the first thing that comes to mind in the space provided below.

CHAPTER FIVE

"Who are my family & friends?"

I really don't want to break it to you, but you need to know that a lot of your friendships that you have made whilst in school aren't made to last forever.

Whilst your young and don't have the responsibilities of adulthood, by all means enjoy these times to their fullest. Because as you move on and into your working lives, a lot of these relationships will be maintained on social media or may never be maintained at all.

It saddens me to read that the world thinks that young people are too busy hiding behind their mobile devices as opposed to interacting with others face-to-face. I understand that a lot of our day-to-day lives do happen online, however it is crucial that you still maintain who you are when dealing with others in real life situations.

Life can sometimes be confronting and won't always be comfortable, however you still want to make sure that your actively engaged and present within each of these moments. Please remember that again, it is how you react to these situations that will define your character and how others may then go on to perceive you.

In saying that, you should aim to go through life with three different circles of friends. And as I explain these circles to you, you will begin to understand why.

The first circle, are those one or two people that you are really close with. These are the people that you can tell anything to and that you are never embarrassed or feel uncomfortable around. These two people should inspire you, motivate you and support you no matter what. They should never bring you down and they should always have your best interests at heart, just as you with them.

The second circle, is for that group of people that you can catch up with or be around and still have a good time with but don't have to discuss your private life with. These are the people whom you enjoy their company but would never class as a best-friend. There will be many of these people that come and go throughout your lives and it is important that you never over-express yourself within this second or third group as the trust just is not there.

The third circle, is for those people whose paths you will cross in your day to day life. These will be people that you go to school with, see out and about, and eventually those people who you will go on to work with. These people still demand respect just as the others, but these are the ones where your conversations usually revolve around the latest news or what you did on the weekend. Again, the trust just is not there with this group so never over-express yourself with any of these encounters.

As you can now see from the above aside from your friends, your family now becomes really important. If you have a healthy relationship with your family now, in your adult years you will always have the additional support you may need and this can sometimes be crucial as life will throw you some hard times every now and again.

From my experience and whilst in school, I had more than enough friends. However now as an adult, my best friend is someone that I never even knew in school and all of those people that I went to school with, well I don't even hear from anymore.

If I'm not spending time with my own family now (my wife and kids), you can usually find me spending time with my parents or my brothers. Because as you get older, you realize that family is important and that you should really make more of an effort to be apart of each other's lives.

Please just think about this for a moment and how your life may be different if you only had certain people in it. Don't let people discourage you from being all that you were intended to be. And definitely don't let people influence you into doing something or partaking in an activity that you are not happy to be a part of.

CHAPTER FIVE

"Challenge"

If you wish, you can follow my own example below and write down some of the people that currently encourage you and why.

This helps to really understand why you may respect that person and why you would like to maintain a positive relationship with them moving forward.

This could even be a "High Profile Personality" such as an Author, Celebrity or Sportsman.

It's important to always be surrounded by those people that inspire you to believe in yourself and encourage you to want to achieve more for your life.

People that currently encourage me and inspire me to believe in myself are,

(My Example)

1. My Parents because they are always encouraging and supportive with everything that I do. Even if they don't always understand why I do them.

2. Kevin Hart (Celebrity) because I can appreciate how he came from nothing and has now built himself up into a household name. I like his work ethic, his drive and sense of ambition.

3. Tony Robbins (Author & Motivational Speaker) because he is full of wisdom and when I listen to him speak or read one of his books, it inspires me to want to change and to become better.

Please fill in the blank spaces with your answers for those people that currently encourage and inspire you to believe in yourself.

(Your Answers)

1. ……………….. because …

2. ……………….. because …

3. ……………….. because …

If you would prefer, rather than write down the names of people as above you could write down the different personality traits that you are both drawn to and away from.

These could be things like my example below, however I would encourage you to take the time and to complete this exercise as I believe it will help you achieve more clarity with the personality types that you would prefer to go on to do life with as an adult.

It is important to note that a "Personality Trait" is a specific characteristic that a person may have. They can be either positive or negative.

On the following page is a list of some positive personality traits to give you an example,

Positive Personality Traits,

Affectionate	Hard-Working	Sensitive
Ambitious (motivated)	Honest	Serious
Aspiring	Humble	Sincere
Accepts/Embraces Change	Interested	Sympathetic
Caring	Jealous	Thoughtful
Cheerful	Kind	Trusting
Considerate	Mature	Willing
Courageous	Open-Minded	
Courteous	Optimistic/Positive	
Decisive	Practical	
Devoted	Punctual	
Determined	Realistic	
Enthusiastic	Reliable	
Faithful	Respectful	
Forgiving	Responsible	
Friendly	Self-Confident	
Generous	Self-Disciplined	
Grateful	Selfless	

On the following page is a list of some negative personality traits to give you an example,

Negative Personality Traits,

Arrogant	Lazy	Unfriendly
Cold/Distant	Mean	Ungrateful
Constricting	Negative	Unhelpful
Controlling	Pessimistic	Unreliable
Dishonest	Petty	Untrusting
Fearful	Rude	Unwilling
Gives Up	Secretive	
Gloomy	Self-Centered	
Grumpy	Selfish	
Guarded	Small-Minded	
Ignorant/Rejecting	Stubborn	
Immature	Suspicious	
Inconsiderate	Thoughtless	
Indecisive	Uncaring	
Insecure	Undependable	
Insensitive	Unenthusiastic	
Jealous	Unfocussed	
Lack of Faith	Unforgiving	

This is my example for Personality Traits that I am Drawn To …

1. Positivity   *Why? Because I don't want to be around negative people.*

2. Confidence   *Why? Because I want to feel comfortable in my own body and understand that we are all individual and unique.*

3. Ambition   *Why? Because I love to dream big and think outside of the box. I love to be challenged and want more out of life.*

This is my example for Personality Traits that I am Drawn From …

1. Negative   *Why? Because I always want to see the positive and be happy in any/all situations.*

2. Fearful   *Why? Because I believe that anything is possible.*

3. Small-Minded   *Why? Because only I can create my destiny and I want to believe that all my hard work will one day be rewarded.*

You may find that you have more than three, however let's start with the three that stand out in your mind as you can always add to your list later on.

It's important to just make a start and to prepare your mind to think about what's important to you right now.

(Please fill in the blank spaces with your answers for those Personality Traits that you are Drawn To...)

1.   Why?

2.   Why?

3.   Why?

(Please fill in the blank spaces with your answers for those Personality Traits that you are Drawn Away From...)

1.   Why?

2.   Why?

3.   Why?

CHAPTER SIX

"Why Money Matters"

If you are not thinking about it much now, as you move into adulthood money will always be somewhere in the back of your mind.

Managing money is a skill that most of us are not taught from a young age and it is something that I believe should be discussed with you prior to leaving school.

Some of you may already be working a part-time job outside of school and if not, well I would encourage you to do so. Not only does making your own money provide you with a sense of responsibility and a greater understanding, but having a part-time job now within an area of interest may benefit you when going on to secure a full-time position.

They say that it can take 21 days to form a new habit and the way you are spending your money now really should be looked at so that you can create healthier ways of spending if needed.

You can make a note of the things that you currently spend your money on and also of the impact that this may have.

For example,

I currently buy my lunch each day which costs me around $10.00

If I were to save that money, I would have $50.00 at the end of each week which could be saved or used for ...

Good money habits are hard to come by and you really want to grasp these now so that when your an adult and taking care of your own responsibilities, you never fall into debt which has it's own amount of pain and stress.

You should have clear short-term and long-term goals for your money. And you should always have a clear and concise budget for the money you may be making and for the money that you are spending.

When buying your next purchase, try to consider your "needs" verse your "wants."

If you need something then by all means, that should qualify as a valid purchase. However if you are buying things just because you want them, well there is reason to reconsider.

If this is the case, it would be a good idea to sit on that purchase for a few days and if after that time has passed and you still want the item then go ahead and buy it. However you may just find that 90% of the time, once you think about going back to buy that item you have since changed your mind and the money is better saved or spent on something else.

As I am not claiming to be a financial advisor or even an expert in this area, I just wanted to highlight some valuable pieces of advice. For those of you wanting to learn more about managing your money, I would ask that you speak with your parents, teacher or go online for some further guidance and further information.

CHAPTER SEVEN

"Affirmations"

Lastly, I have one more exercise for you to do that is going to seal the deal so to speak.

Affirmations are a great way of inspiring change and starting the transformation process.

We each behave the way that we think and affirmations are a great way for giving you that kick in pants that we tend to need every now and again to stay on track.

I personally use affirmations all the time. I have them written down in notebooks, on post-it notes and sometimes will even write them on my bathroom mirror as constant reminders to achieve my current goals.

Affirmations are going to ensure that you continue to remain in the right state of mind and that you are well and truly on your path to achieving personal greatness!

I recommend starting with ten, however I know people that will go nuts and write up to fifty at a time. Your affirmations should be a reflection of who you are, what you want to become and most importantly, what you need to hear to get there.

They will change as your goals change, and they are the perfect motivator to keep you on track and mentally on point.

So let's get into the last exercise of the book.

CHAPTER SEVEN

"Challenge"

An example of some affirmations that you could use are,

1. *I am strong.*

2. *I am smart.*

3. *I am worthy.*

4. *I am grateful.*

5. *I am unique.*

6. *I am kind and I inspire others.*

7. *I am capable of things greater than myself.*

8. *I am in control of my destiny and choose who I become.*

9. *I am committed to remaining focused and to achieving my goals.*

10. I have the power to change my story, regardless of my past.

11. I have the power to build the life I want.

12. I love my body and appreciate my flaws.

13. I make healthy decisions for my body.

14. I will always seek to learn and grow.

15. I am positive, persistent and I will never quit.

Please now take the time to complete your own list of affirmations on the space provided below.

(Your Answers)

1.

2.

3.

4.

5.

6.

7.

8.

9.

10.

CHAPTER EIGHT

"The Blueprint"

Congratulations! Now that we have gone through and clearly defined what our personal goals are, we can begin to move forward in the right direction to defining what areas we are interested in and may now want to actively pursue as a career once finishing school.

If you were to go back and read through each of your "Chapter Challenges" the answers which you have completed will now highlight a clear and well outlined path that you have written out for yourself to now follow.

Your answers and this book, now form your very own "Blueprint".

This is valuable information because when it comes to choosing a career or field of study, you can look at the options within these areas of interest and you will be destined to go on to do great things whilst living a healthy and balanced lifestyle.

It really doesn't matter if your answers seem too big or too small right now, what matters is that you have started the process in understanding who it is that you would like to become.

It would also be a great idea to find some people that have gone before you and achieved their own success in these area's as this is great motivation and insight as to what it is that you may have to do in order to achieve your own results within these fields.

This is what I would refer to as the "Shadow Technique", and you will want to research and follow those people, whether it be either in-person or on a social media platform as these are the ones who have already done the work and may be achieving your desired results.

If you too can apply the same principles, do the work and commit to your goals, then you can achieve the same results or even go one better.

This means that you must all become forward-thinkers, world changers and have the ability to think outside of the box. You see, from this perspective you can do anything that you put your mind to. And I strongly believe that!

I would also encourage you to use your answers alongside your weekly schedule, as this helps to better manage your time and to not waste anymore of it. If you don't currently work to a schedule, I would encourage you to start doing so.

Allocate your time according to your new "Blueprint" and be sure to include time each day for those around you. This could be a little bit of trial and error to begin with but believe me, it will be one of the best things you could ever do.

"Dreams are achievable, but you have to believe that it is possible and you must be willing to do the work!

- Markus De Silva

CHAPTER NINE

"The To Do List"

It's now time for you to get creative with your answers and to come up with your own vision board, so that moving forward you are able to see what motivates you on a daily basis.

Remember, "You are your own inspiration!" So don't hold back and make your vision board as bright and as colourful as you wish to suit your individual personality.

Encourage and motivate one another to pursue greatness. Never discredit your self-worth and what you are capable of going on to achieve.

Once you have this completed, hang it up on a wall at home so that it is one of the first things you see every morning and also one of the last things you see each evening before going to bed.

Words have power, so recite your affirmations daily and don't stop believing in yourself!

Next, lets take our goal setting to the next level.

It's great that we have previously written out some of our goals in Chapter Seven, however a goal needs to measurable and this happens when we allocate it a timeframe for completion.

I am going to show you the same process that I currently use for goal setting and that is as follows,

In order for me to ….., I need to …

I will achieve this by …... before the …

An example of how this could be used is,

In order for me to leave school and become a Zoo-Keeper, I need to research the criteria and courses available.

I will achieve this by searching online, contacting Universities and speaking to my Guidance Counsellor at school. I will have this mapped out before the end of Term 2.

Another example could be,

In order for me to be happy, I need to feel confident within myself.

I will achieve this by starting to workout for 30-45 minutes every Monday/Wednesday/Friday for the next four weeks starting from Monday the 00/00/0000.

Remember, these are just examples, however you can measure your goals in other ways to suit.

Lastly, I want to encourage you all to find an "Accountability Partner" whilst pursuing your blueprint and this could either be a willing Parent, Friend or even a Teacher.

This person needs to know what it is that you are setting out to achieve, why you want to achieve it and when you would like to achieve it by.

It may also be helpful to come up with a reward system, so that once you have completed a goal or objective within your blueprint, you can celebrate the occasion and record your milestones.

This process should be repeated with each of your goals until you have completed your list.

As you get older and your goals change, you can use these same techniques within this book to go on and to achieve your new goals/aspirations as well.

CHAPTER TEN

"Final Thoughts"

It is my goal to empower you all to find a clear sense of what it is that you are both interested in and may want to pursue after leaving High School.

I hope that this book has been able to help you achieve this through my own journey and with the exercises that I have set out for you within the "Chapter Challenges" of this book.

I would strongly encourage you to sit down regularly and to review and to discuss your results with your parents and your teachers. This process will enable you to seek some guidance as to what the next steps may be that you can now take to be actively moving forward into securing either further study or a permanent full-time position within an industry that highly interests you.

I would like to think that you would take the lessons learnt and your answers seriously. I would hate for you to waste any of your adult lives working in positions that don't offer you any reward or any job satisfaction.

Please take a page out of the books from the rest of us who have gone before you and now really think about what it is that you may want to do. And whilst your still in school, please make the effort to actively engage with those resources available to you in order to achieve these goals.

If I could give you all just one more piece of encouragement it would be this,

"You do have what it takes. You are more than capable. And I believe in YOU!"

- Markus De Silva

ABOUT THE AUTHOR

Markus De Silva is passionate about empowering others to achieve a healthy outlook to life by giving them an opportunity to create a blueprint for their lives. This enables them to be happy with who they are, whilst on the path to becoming who they want to be.

Markus lives in Perth, Australia. He loves spending time with his family, writing and going fishing.

Other titles available by this Author

"The Fundamental Four"
Empowering you to find balance within your
Health, Family, Work & Fun.

"Hearing Dad for the First Time"

These titles are available on Amazon & other selected Retailers.

Notes